PSEUDO
DISCIPLESHIP

PSEUDO
DISCIPLESHIP

By: George Verwer

LITERATURE

FOREWORD

The message of this book was originally presented to a conference of young people taking part in Operation Mobilization crusades, in Europe.

This penetrating message by George Verwer deserves a wider audience, and this little book will surely make many of us *uncomfortable* —because sooner or later we will recognize ourselves in some of the characters of PSEUDO-DISCIPLESHIP!

However, some doubters may ask if there really are such people as false or pseudo-disciples. *Unfortunately, it is only too possible!*

And if we do find a rather unflattering picture of ourselves in this book, then let us not try to cover it up, but let us face up honestly to the indictment, surrendering every area of our lives to the One who alone can cleanse away the hidden hypocrisies, and make us His true disciples.

Actually, most readers will recognize that the list of pseudo-disciples in this book is not altogether complete. Sadly, there are others, among them **Mr. Half-Truth.**

We discover this particular pseudo-disciple by the strange way he frequently describes a situation in such a way as to strengthen his own deductions. Or, in speaking of others, especially those he does not like so much, he repeats only those nuggets of information which confirm his own unpleasant suspicions.

Mr. Half-Truth, who is, of course, first cousin to **Mr. Liar,** dislikes the whole truth because he is usually an extremist, with a strong negative *bias* about many people and ideas.

His dismal relative, **Mr. Innuendo,** is more clever and subtle. His chosen words, even his very tone, suggest a lot, and seldom anything very good, either! He doesn't believe in *open attack*—Oh, no! He uses a technique of the devil who asked: "Has God said . . .?"

And so, it is hard to remember what **Mr. Innuendo** actually says, but when he is gone, the mind of the listener is left in doubt and mistrust concerning others, so that ugly suspicions arise which may divide the closest of friends!

Mr. Innuendo's close friend, **Mr. Talebearer,** is one who cheerfully and deliberately repeats those interesting stories about other believers. He does this because his juicy tidbits of news will usually guarantee some brief attention at least—*but at what a cost!*

His talebearing often damages the reputation of others, and spoils many friendships (Proverbs 11:12, 13 and 17: 9).

Easy to read, this book has touches of humor, but it carries with it a sword thrust that will strike into many hearts. May it cause us to examine our own lives and believe God to cleanse away those things which are not pleasing to Him, that we may follow the One who has called us to walk the way of true discipleship.

—THE PUBLISHERS

PSEUDO-DISCIPLESHIP

We have heard much about what a disciple *is,* but in this message I want to speak about what a disciple is *not!*

There are many in our day who pretend to be disciples. Always within our own ranks there are those who either pretend to be disciples, or who are deceived into thinking they *are* disciples. Could it be that even in the ranks of a group where the workers receive no salaries and preach Christ supposedly because they love Him, there could be pseudo-disciples?

Yes, without a doubt it is possible, and I am convinced that it is God's desire to purge every true work of His, of false disciples.

Let's read *Acts 5:1-11:*

But in another case, a man named Ananias (with his wife Sapphira) sold some property, and brought only part of the money, claiming it was the full price. (Sapphira had agreed to this deception). But Peter said, "Ananias, Satan has filled your heart! When you claimed this was the full price, you were lying to the Holy Spirit. The property was yours to sell or not, as you wished. And after selling it, it was yours to decide how much to give. How could you do a thing like this? You weren't lying to us, but to God."

As soon as Ananias heard these words, he fell to the floor dead! Everyone was terrified, and the younger men covered him with a sheet and took him out and buried him.

> About three hours later his wife came in, not knowing what had happened. Peter asked her, "Did you people sell your land for such and such a price?" "Yes," she said, "we did." And Peter said, "How could you and your husband even think of doing a thing like this — conspiring together to test the Spirit of God's ability to know what is going on? Just outside that door are the young men that buried your husband, and they will carry you out too."
>
> Instantly she fell to the floor dead, and the young men came in and, seeing she was dead, carried her out and buried her beside her husband. Terror gripped the entire church and all others who heard what had happened.*

Notice that Ananias and Sapphira were not obliged to give their land. There were no rules about giving all. There were no pressures put on the believers to sell all. Their sin was not they did not give all, but rather that they were pretending to be what they *knew* they were not, pretending in order to receive the praise and recognition of men. God took them as an example for His church in all ages, including the Twentieth Century. If God worked that way today, our churches and possibly this very hall tonight would be full of corpses!

What impresses me in verse eleven is that, as a result of God's action, great fear came upon the church. I have observed that in our day the fear of God is very rare. In this perverse generation, the majority dare to presume that God would never punish for sin in this age of grace. We have had young people in our summer crusades living blatantly hypocritical lives. We have had a few young people with us for an entire year whose lives we discovered were nothing but sham. They lied to their leaders, they lied to me, they lied to their own parents and churches. Thank God, there have been very few such cases. But those few have convinced me that attending conferences, listening to the messages of men of God, participating in a program of evangelism, etc., is no guarantee against the subtle snares of pseudo-discipleship.

How anyone could attend a conference like some of ours have been and not understand the way of repentance and brokenness is beyond me. But it can happen. "The heart is deceitful and desperately wicked. Who can know it?" (Jeremiah 17:9).

And so I want to ask that all of us be willing to let the spotlight of God come upon each one of us individually. Please forget, if you will, the other person. It is not for you to shine the spotlight upon your wife or your husband, your friend or your leader. I pray that we will each let the spotlight shine directly on our own life, and with all my heart I want to let it shine full force on me.

The pseudo-disciple pretends to be a learner, but he is not. He has all the outward signs, and many are fooled by him. But he is a fake, a counterfeit. He takes part in all the meetings, he sings, he prays, he evangelizes, he sells books, he reads his Bible. But basically his life is not compatible with the principles of discipleship which Christ laid down.

I have listed twenty-one pseudo-disciples. We will not be able to touch on all of them, but let's consider some of them, beginning with **Mr. Liar.** We might just as well begin here, taking our example straight from Scripture; Ananias and Sapphira were liars. We see from their example that it is possible to be living nominally as a Christian, appearing to

follow Christ, taking an active part in Christian community, and yet be a liar. There have been a few among us who, after some time, confessed to lying on their questionnaire, perhaps about age, perhaps about something in their past which they were afraid would leak out. "How is that possible among Christians?" you ask. But really, the longer you live among Christians the more you will realize that it *is* possible! *The heart is deceitful and desperately wicked!*

Let's be realistic. I wonder if anyone here is in that category tonight? Living a lie! Telling lies, convenient lies, white lies . . . they are the same thing, no matter what the situation. The Bible says, "all liars will have their part" . . . where? . . . "in the lake of fire!" I tell you, lying is a dangerous business, and eventually . . . *eventually* . . . the truth will find you out!

Older and wiser brother to Mr Liar is **Mr. Deceiver**. He is a specialist! He doesn't engage in those straightforward, crusty lies. He likes the "around-the-corner" variety. He is a master at giving false impressions. He is often guilty of exaggeration. Perhaps all his life he has craved love and attention, and he finds that when he exaggerates, people listen to him. No one seems very

interested in the plain old truth *("I gave out a hundred tracts")*; but oh, how people flock around him when he puts a little glow on the story *("I gave out a thousand tracts, and wow! in only one hour!")*

Of course, we are all guilty of this from time to time, because we have a sinful nature. But there is a difference between those who are blatantly guilty before God, knowingly practising sin, and those who fall into it unawares in an unguarded moment. I would not classify these latter with Mr. Deceiver, but whether it is habitual, or whether it is sudden and unpremeditated, exaggeration is sin of which we must repent. It is so easy for subtle deceit to enter the picture. You are in your room praying, and you have fallen asleep on your knees. Someone enters the room and you wake up suddenly and say, "Amen," as if you were deep in prayer. Ever done that? Or you are sitting at your desk munching a nice chocolate bar. There comes a knock on the door, and, whoosh, into the drawer goes the chocolate bar! Some think that these little ways of deceiving are sharp and shrewd. God says that they are sin. He tells us that we are to walk *honestly* before men. In Psalm 51 we find that He "desireth truth in the inward parts." Oh, that God will drive that home to our hearts!

Another pseudo-disciple who is never far away is **Mr. Fault-Finder.** Just as soon as he makes his appearance, you can be sure he will give you a good

headache, because he sees everything that is wrong . . . well, all except what is wrong with himself!

He feels that he is a real follower of Christ and that he is really doing a great job for Him. But when he looks around at the others (and he is *always* looking around at the others) all he finds is immaturity, lack of experience, lack of leadership ability, emotional problems . . . and so he goes on. He thinks he is following Jesus, but does not realize that his very attitude disqualifies him from following closely after the Lord.

Mr. Fault-Finder is sometimes called by his other name, **Mr. Judge-Others.** He fixes on some little detail, and immediately he puts two and two together and four and four together, but the trouble is that when he adds it all up he gets the wrong answer. There is such a danger in Christian work of judging others — other groups, other individuals. And God hates that! This pseudo-disciple is convinced that he is following Jesus, but he is off on a wide tangent that leads to a deep ditch.

An enthusiastic pseudo-disciple who sometimes makes his way into Christian work is **Mr. Runaway.** He bursts in with great zeal, shouting,

"I've been called to China!" and everyone stands back amazed.

Well, we discover a bit later that he has not been called to China, or to any other country. He has only felt a "call" to run away from something — a home situation, a job failure, a girl who dropped him, or some other unpleasant situation that he does not want to face. Christian service seems like a wonderful escape. Here is a great opportunity, an open door, inviting him to escape from his frustrations and fears and difficult circumstances.

Mr. Runaway is not a disciple. And if he feels that he must run away from the unpleasant, he will be running all his life. It may be that God will want him to return to that very situation and see victory in it, or it *could* be that God will want him to repent of his false motivation and press on from here with true motivation.

I can see how God worked this way in my life. I came to Jesus with false motives. When I was born again in 1955, I didn't go down the aisle of Madison Square Gardens because I loved God. I didn't go because I wanted to be a worshipper of Him and give Him all I had. Not at all! I went down the aisle because I was broken and burdened by my sin and I wanted deliverance and forgiveness. That is pretty selfish, isn't it? Most of us, in fact, came to Christ for selfish reasons — how else could He draw the unregenerate man to Himself? because before he knows Christ he has no pure motives. But once he becomes a Christian, God can modify them. If there is some circumstance in your life you want to run away from, God can use it to draw you to Himself.

It is important, however, that you do not allow false motivation to continue. You may have come to Christ for the wrong reasons, but you should never try to serve Him for the wrong reasons. Running away never solved any problem; running to God always provides an answer.

There is another pseudo-disciple who is seen very frequently within our ranks — **Mr. Girl-Hunter**. Whaaaat?! Here? Yes, and **Miss Husband-Hunter**, too! They like to think they are following Jesus whatever the cost. But really, they are following the twitterings of their own hearts. Mr. Girl-Hunter meets a girl during the summer gospel crusade, and she says, "I'm going on tour for a year."

"My," he said, "isn't that a coincidence? The Lord has been leading me that way as well."

He thinks he is following Jesus, but really he is following *her*. He is led astray by the deceitfulness of his own heart.

With Miss Husband-Hunter, maybe it started back in her own church the first time she heard the work presented — when that good-looking young man got up and said, "Come on tour for a year and serve the Lord." It sounded so terrific . . . especially the way *he* said it! She thought (not consciously, of course), "Well, maybe I'll never get a chance with him, but if there is one, there must be more."

We are usually not aware of such thoughts because they occur in our subconscious minds. That is why God wants to shine the spotlight of His Word right down to the depths of our subconscious. That is why we must hide the Word in our hearts, study it, meditate on it, digest it; so that it might get down deep into the inner man — *the real self.*

God will not allow you to share your love for Him with anybody else, so make sure, young people, that you are following Jesus and not some fellow or girl. The Lord may give you a wife. Wonderful! He may give you a husband. Praise Him! The Bible says, "The man who finds a wife finds a good thing" (Proverbs 18:22). But let it be

* *The Living Psalms and Proverbs*

God who brings you a husband or a wife, and not *you* who goes out looking for one! He is far more capable of choosing the one who is best for you than you are!

The next pseudo-disciple to come along is **Mr. Shortcut**. He truly has a vision for the mission field and wants to see the world bombarded with the

gospel of Christ. He spots us through his binoculars, sees all these young people going off to evangelize, and he says, "That's for me!"

He had thought about going to college . . . but oh, that takes four years! He had thought about Bible College, but it would take a chunk out of his life, and he is already 18. He has considered many things, but they all take so long and he just can't wait.

Operation Mobilization seems to him the ideal thing — a shortcut to discipleship! A shortcut to world evangelism! But unfortunately the shortcut often turns out to be the longest road.

We must realize, young people, that there is no shortcut in accomplishing things for God. This has been our belief from the beginning of this work. Remember, this work is not a mission board, but a training program meant to give experience and preparation to young men and women, so that after a couple of years (maybe even six or seven years), they can go out as missionaries, sent by their local assembly or church, or by some mission society.

Many young people who have been on previous crusades and have really understood the purpose of O.M. are now in university or Bible College. They discovered that one or two years with O.M. gives them something for which to work when they return to college or higher education.

I do not mean to imply by this that after O.M. everyone should return to college. Each person is different. If we would only realize that you cannot put everyone in the same mold. The great cry today is, "Everybody to Bible College." DRUUUMMM, DUM, DUM! Everybody off to Bible College like a bunch of tin soldiers. You just cannot serve Christ if you have not been to Bible College!!

I praise God that I graduated from one, but I certainly do not believe that everyone who wants to serve Christ *must* go to Bible College. I do believe that everyone who wants to serve Christ must go to *God's* college, whatever it might be. It might be in the mechanic's shop or the literature department. It might be at the typewriter or in the kitchen. Or it might be learning at the feet of a man of God. This seems to me a bit more scriptural than some of the methods we are using today.

We must realize that there are no shortcuts to the kind of life that Jesus Christ meant for us. It is a long, hard road, and we are all just leaners. Think of the Roman Catholic priest who studies nine years before he is ordained, or think of the medical student who studies for seven years before he can set up practice as a doctor, often postponing marriage and a home because medicine comes first. But we sometimes have a Mr. Shortcut with us who feels that after one year with O.M. he is ready to turn the world upside down. Actually, he can hardly get up on time!

Mr. Shortcut is a pseudo-disciple who is unwilling to pay the price and persevere. He is continually jumping from one place to another, and makes no impact anywhere. Young people, do not look for a shortcut. There is none for a life that is going to count. *Never sacrifice the permanent on the altar of the immediate.*

Next we meet **Mr. Sluggard.** Billy Graham names slothfulness as one of the seven deadly sins, and it is certainly one of the most common which I

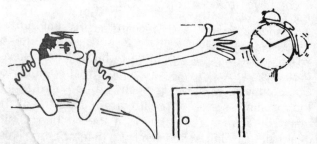

see in our day. Think of the prophet Nehemiah, and those people who had a mind to work (Nehemiah

4:6) — where are this kind of men today? Think about the virtuous woman of Proverbs 31, who did her work early in the morning before anyone was up and was still going late at night by the light of her candle — where is this kind of girl today?

Proverbs 26:13 gives us a picture of the sluggard: "The lazy man won't go out and work. 'There might be a lion outside!' he says." *

Funny, isn't it? Now I don't think it is very likely that there really was a lion in the streets. The truth is, the man is lazy and sees only the obstacles.

You say, "Let's press on." But he says, "Oh, we have to get our rest." You say, "Let's move out from house to house." But he says, " It's pretty cold today. We might catch cold."

For every suggestion he has a "But . . . if . . . no . . . can't." He has ninety-nine negatives for every positive step forward, but the real problem is that he is lazy. Proverbs 20:4 says, "The sluggard will not plow by reason of the cold." I would like to paraphrase that verse: "The O.M.'er will not go door to door by reason of the rain." One sub-zero day in Austria the leader says, "Let's go, troops, out on the doors!" Mr. Sluggard begins shaking and quivering and says, "Don't you think we should have a little extra Bible study today?" What a grievous thing it is when we use Bible study as an excuse for laziness. I see it all over the evangelical world.

The man in the secular world gets up at 6:30 a.m. and is on his job, working hard at 8:00 a.m. But the evangelical? Well, he is in "full-time"

* The Living Psalms and Proverbs

Christian work and so he gets up at 7:30 or 8:00, has a leisurely breakfast, followed by a two-hour Bible study. Is this right, young people? To have a two-hour Bible study is an excellent plan *if* we are intensively studying with the purpose of letting the Word of God mold our lives. But it is *not* right if we are relaxing in our favorite armchair with our Bible in our hands, merely reading and lethargically looking out the window from time to time. Reading without taking notes is simply an invitation to sleep. Our Bible study should not be an ingenious subconscious excuse to get out of work — but rather an intensive, exhausting mental and spiritual experience! What an insult it is to God to fall asleep reading His Word! Can you imagine my sitting here face to face with Jesus Christ, and as He talks to me I begin to yawn and say drowsily, "Isn't that tremendous, Lord?". . . and then I fall asleep! *And this is what happens.* What mockery to God the way we sometimes have our quiet time. If you tend to grow sleepy during Bible study, try walking around and memorizing a little. John Wesley used to study his Bible on horseback as he traveled across England from one open air meeting to another.

Look at Proverbs 20:13 —"Love not sleep, lest thou come to proverty; open thine eyes and thou shalt be satisfied with bread."

We have been discovering that with a group as immature as we are, it is good to have to knock on doors, and "keep going," carrying a heavy bookbag and earning our daily keep. It is the greatest tent-making business we can engage in. If the Apostle Paul was not ashamed to make tents and sell them, dare any of us be ashamed to go out and sell Christian books to earn at least a bit of our support, so that the few gifts that come our way can be channeled to more strategic people? — to those faithful Indians, Mexicans, Spaniards and Italians who can speak the language! Let *them* go out and do the personal work. Let *us* support them with our money and prayers!

God give us a vision for tent-making. Let us be zealous in all we attempt, and not be deceived into thinking that we are disciples when *our life* says we are sluggards.

Mr. Sluggard has a very close friend, about whom I will say only a little. He is **Mr. Little-As-Possible.** He rides into O.M. headquarters in the

back of a truck, and is the first one out. Someone else will unload the truck and clean it out, so he goes and has a chat with his friends. Mr. Little-As-Possible volunteers occasionally for the washing-up (especially when he sees that the girl he has his eye on has volunteered). But he only manages to get the plates and cups and cutlery washed. He puts the pots and pans to one side to soak and never remembers to wipe the crumbs off the table or clean the stove. If only we could exchange Mr. Little-As-Possible for a *Mr. Much-As-Possible!* Oh for some *Extra-Mile* men. These are the ones who do *more* than they are asked to do, and if they are not asked to do it, they do it anyway. These are the ones I want on my team. We have had them on our O.M. teams, many of them, and I tell you every one of them thrills my heart. They are a rebuke to my life.

But here comes another pseudo-disciple:

Mr. Halfway. He cannot wait — "Let's go, start the race!" *Vroommm!* And he is off and away, ahead of everyone else. People look at him and

think he is a sure winner — such energy, such speed. But halfway around the track he begins huffing and puffing and then, "My, it's a long way to the end . . . just don't think I can make it. Maybe I've made a mistake?'' And he comes to a grinding halt, and looks for another race.

Have you ever begun something you didn't finish? Silly question! *We all have.* It would be interesting to know how much money we invested last year in Navigator Courses for young people who had a great burst of zeal for Bible memorization. Many of them are still on the second packet. It is false zeal, and when the energy of the flesh has exhausted itself, this zeal will be no more!

Now let's meet **Miss Successful.** Her whole joy is in doing her job well, because when she completes it, it gives her a great feeling of accomplishment, and of course brings her recognition and praise as well.

Do you enjoy that feeling of accomplishment? Psychologists would say, "Of course, it is necessary for human happiness and well-being. One who has no *sense of accomplishment* will end up in a mental home." It is true that God often allows us to have a feeling of accomplishment, but unless we present the work accomplished to Him, and give Him all the glory for having enabled us to do it, then I am afraid that it will be included in the wood, hay, and stubble on the Day of Judgment. It is self-produced zeal which so often works fervently, simply to be able to say, "I have finished the job! I am a success!"

Miss Successful is at her best when others of the group are working close by, especially if a good-looking fellow is giving out tracts across the street from her. And, on her own for a day of book-selling, she puts everything she has into it, and really excels. She feels terrific, just bubbling over with her success when she meets the group that evening. She is feeling so happy, in fact, she does not even realize how much all her glowing stories discourage the quiet girl on the team who has been faithfully knocking on the doors all day with no outward signs of success. In actual fact, young people, it is often this timid girl who has quietly committed her work unto the Lord who is the *real* Miss Successful, spiritually speaking.

Next on the list are **Mr. Know-It-All** and **Mr. Teach-Me-Not.** These pseudo-disciples are very plentiful. Mr. Know-It-All says, "I know how to put

that tent up. You just get out of the way a minute." And his brother says, "That's right. Look, you can't tell us anything about camping. We've done it all our lives. We have experience." We often discover these twins among the older folk. Now, I am aware that the older generation feels that all the problems lie in us, and I think we realize that we are often guilty and must bend and break and repent. But, oh, how it thrills my heart to meet a pastor, an elder, a missionary who is willing to admit that he *might* be wrong, that there still might be *one* lesson he can learn before he gets to Glory — and who is humble enough to be willing to learn it from a young person, if God so desires. Believe me, I want to learn all I can while I am young, but if I live to be a hundred I want to keep on learning and bending and breaking until the day I go to meet my Lord.

These twins find their way onto almost all of the O.M. teams and make life generally unpleasant for the rest. I would be so happy to send them home where they would no doubt be appreciated for all their experience and knowledge. One thing is certain about them: they are sure to quench the Holy Spirit in their lives by their unteachable spirit.

One pseudo-disciple who is just clamoring for acknowledgment is **Mr. Noise-Maker.** You can usually find him in a prayer meeting, punctuating

every other word with a constant stream of ''Amen's,'' ''Hallelujah's,'' etc. Now there is nothing wrong with a good shout of genuine praise (and we have probably more people on the other end of the pendulum who wouldn't let loose.a shout of praise if they saw a man jump out of the grave!) but.if you are a Mr. Noise-Maker, you had better be careful, for God might just test the genuineness of your noise.

"Praise the Lord!" you shout when you find a pencil that you lost. *What do you mean by that?* Are you really offering praise to the Lord, or is it just a little Christian slang expression you throw around lightly? "Amen!" you say when someone prays, "Lord, I believe you for five thousand souls this year in Italy." Do you *really* believe it? Be careful what you "amen" in a prayer.

Why, in some of our prayer meetings you can almost hear Satan's strongholds crumbling in the background, but then a month later, when there isn't quite the same "atmosphere," when perhaps some discouragements have been experienced or you haven't heard any stirring messages recently, then when the time for the prayer meeting comes the only noise to be heard is the low moan of a group of discouraged little would-be Christian disciples. Let us be careful that our discipleship does not end with noise . . . words . . . sounds . . . that fade away in the noise of battle.

Search your heart and count the cost until, by God's grace, you are convinced that when the day of trial and difficulty or heartache comes, *you will be making the same noise!* There is nothing wrong with a good shout, a good "Amen!" But don't praise God only when you are "on top." Be prepared to praise Him just as much when you are down in the valley. *He has not changed just because your spirits are low.*

The next pseudo-disciple is rather stubborn — he is **Mr. Doctrine-Pusher.** You are likely to meet Mr. Noise-Maker pretty quickly but Mr. Doctrine-

Pusher is rather quiet at first, especially when someone is around who is well grounded in the Word. He comes out of his hiding once he has identified those hungry Christians who really want to get to know the Word more thoroughly. Then he begins to "share" his views on the Word, and he comes up with some of the most interesting doctrines you have ever heard. He prefers to air his views behind the back of the leader, and most of all when he is alone with one or two weaker Christians. He quickly picks out the sincere ones who really want to learn more of God, and he is certain that he is the very one to teach them — he has just the hard core of truth that they need.

There are people who are close to being mentally ill on this point — you just cannot talk to them; you cannot reason with them; you cannot even get on the same wavelength with them. There are some heart-breaking cases of this type — people whose lives are so obviously a sham that everybody knows it, but when you begin to question them on their lives they begin to rave about their pet doctrines; they relate everything to these and nothing will deter them. Most people who get on some doctrinal tangent are people who have def inite psychological problems. The mental institutions of the world are filled with deeply religious, but deceived, people, who suffer from illusions of religious grandeur. But there are also many people like this who are *not* in institutions. Do not be surprised if you find one sitting next to you at church.

Some of the most fantastically fiery preachers I have ever heard in my life were in the southern part of the United States, raving and shouting about some religious obsession they had, and there are things that have been said on radio broadcasts along this line that would knock you off your chair. The United States has more sects and cults and false religions than most pagan countries in the world. There is every possible type of primitive, apostolic, sub-apostolic and super-apostolic group, and the followers of them are almost always absolutely convinced that *they* have the truth. We want no one like this on our teams — people who are determined to air their views and push their own doctrines; they are a hindrance.

The next pseudo-disciple is a close relative of Mr. Doctrine-Pusher. His name is **Mr. Sign-Seeker.** He can never make any decisions without having a definite "sign" from God, and still worse, in every minor detail and circumstance of life he sees a "sign."

If the doorknob falls off in his hand, it is a

sure sign from God that he shouldn't leave the house

that day. When some nice boy happens to open the door for **Miss Sign-Seeker,** she is convinced that he is the one God has for her. If these sign-seekers go for an hour without selling a book, they say God has shown them they should pack up and go home for the day. Mr. Sign-Seeker always has some sensational new story to tell you, and he is usually an ardent follower of some of the spectacular "sign-promoters" of our day.

Frankly, it is a bit difficult for me sometimes to draw the line between "sign" and just plain old superstition!

Beware, young people! The Lord Jesus said, "A wicked and adulterous generation seeketh after a sign; and there shall be no sign given unto it, but the sign of the prophet Jonas" (Matthew 16:4).

The Lord Jesus did not want His disciples to seek after signs but after *Himself;* not after *blessings* but after the *Blesser* — Himself. Why, people will flock from all over the world to a convention when they are told they will receive a blessing. They will fly first class jet from California to New York to receive a blessing. But I have always wondered what would happen if one of these conventions put a sign up saying "Suffering for all." How many would attend then? And yet, doesn't the Word teach, "For unto you it is given in the behalf of Christ, not only to believe on Him, but also to suffer for His sake"

(Philippians 1:29). May God search our hearts on this point.

Next we meet **Mr. Worry-Wart.** He is pressing on and really seems to be going places! He is often very diligent and conscientious, and to see his  puckered brow you would think he is deep in thought. But really, he is deep in worry! He worries about whether he is good enough for God. He worries about whether he is accomplishing enough. He worries about getting his job done on time. He worries about his team members. He worries about the vehicles. He worries about opposition from the police. And on and on and on. And he thinks that worry is an essential part of his life — nothing will be accomplished if he does not worry about it.

But I want to tell you that worry is not a virtue, *it is a sin!* It is the sin which says, "I don't trust you, God — I don't really believe You can take care of this problem. I don't really believe You have permitted this mistake for my good. I don't believe You are absolutely in control!"

The real problem is that Mr. Worry-Wart has not learned to rest in Christ. Let us press on to learn this precious lesson.

Have you met the next pseudo disciple? He is
Mr. Adventurer. He is young and energetic, and
when he hears about Operation Mobilization it

looks like the juiciest
steak he has ever come
across! He has the op-
portunity of crossing
continents at 21 years of
age! He can see the seven
wonders of the world
and take all kinds of
slides and send them
home to his friends, and
learn languages and ride
on camels and—oh, how
exciting!

Oh dear, I feel so sorry for Mr. Adventurer. He
is one of the most disillusioned persons on O.M.
What he thinks is going to be a long, exciting
holiday turns out to be a sort of "pressure" cooker.
True, he may go from England to India, but it will
be in the back of a truck . . . that has no windows
. . . and he will not be able to see anything all the
way, except the faces of his teammates. If he sees
the Taj Mahal at all, he will be giving out tracts so
fast he will hardly notice it. And as for his little
camera, well, he leaves that at home.

I can tell you, young people, it is no adventure
to knock on doors in 120-degree heat all day long.
He may think it is the first week, and the second
and the third. But what about the second *month?*
Soon Mr. Adventurer will be asking for a trip home,

tourist class. And we just do not bring them back from India so soon.

May God drive from us the spirit of adventure and make us count the cost. This is warfare! It will be hard from beginning to end. It will be against your flesh, your culture, your habits! Mr. Adventurer, you need to get off at the first stop.

There is another pseudo-disciple who makes his way into Operation Mobilization every year — **Mr. Freeloader.** "What? They don't even charge you to go on O.M.? That's for me!" And Mr. Freeloader packs his bag and "joins" O.M.

He travels free, he always has at least a few square feet of floor space to sleep on, his meals are provided for him, and all his needs are met.

Yet, strangely enough, it is always a Mr. Freeloader who is the first to complain when a vehicle breaks down or a meal is late. "Terrible living conditions," he says. "Awful food. We should be having meat more often. Our bodies need it!"

He is one of those dual personalities and his other name is Mr. Little-As-Possible. He has a very warped idea that, though he contributes nothing, he should still receive only the best.

Now, it is true that we do not require a tuition or anything in the way of money from you. But does that mean that you are not expected to contribute *anything? No!* This, of course, is grace. But I say to you that grace does over and above the minimum, and I am here to remind you that *you are responsible before God to believe Him to supply your needs!*

You may be young and weak in the faith and feel that you just cannot believe God for anything. But you must start somewhere, and if you just set a small amount before God that you *can* believe Him for, as He provides that, your faith will begin to grow. And I trust that what you cannot believe Him to supply in funds at first, you will make up *in hard work and a disciplined Life.* Then, when God sees that you mean business about this, you will begin to see the funds come in.

The Bible says, "If any would not work, neither should he eat." Remember this, young people, and if you are not disposed to a hard day's work, then please, just do not appear at the meal table.

Oh, that God would put within all Christians a mind to work!

The next young pseudo-disciple is in such a hurry that we hardly have time to meet him! His name is **Mr. Too-Busy.** He knows very little about real discipleship, but he manages to cover it all up with a very busy life. He likes to tell you how busy he is. "Can't possibly do that, I'm too busy. I must

get these letters written . . . no, first I'll make that telephone call . . . or should I first fill these book orders? Oh, dear, so much to do. And then George has asked me to do this and this and this for him . . . you must excuse me.

I have to run." And away he goes, Mr. Too-Busy, like a whirlwind. He is blissfully ignorant that he is the poor victim of an undisciplined and sadly disorganized life. His problem is that he never sits down to organize his jobs and plan the way to accomplish them most efficiently. So he rushes around, unable to decide which are priority jobs and unable to give his full attention to any one of them. Despite his appearance of busyness, he actually accomplishes very little.

Now don't confuse Mr. Too-Busy with **Mr. Busy**. He too has many, many responsibilities, but he is able to take care of them with a minimum of noise and confusion. Both are active. Both walk quickly and have many things to do. But Mr. Too-Busy is always confused and never completes one job without rushing hither and thither, getting more and more panicky as unresolved problems and difficulties pile up on him.

On the other hand, Mr. Busy, although he is in

a hurry, moves quickly but calmly, faithfully taking care of one responsibility as he acquires another.

Let us be careful to make this distinction, because we do not mind at all if Mr. Too-Busy has a little more training in a secular job until he can learn to manage his time a little better. But we are always on the lookout for a Mr. Busy on O.M. I believe that the Spirit of God is desirous of moving us along in world evangelism at something more than a snail's pace, because at the present rate, beloved, we are going rapidly *backwards* in the job of reaching the world for Christ! Some of us need to learn to move a little faster, think faster, concentrate harder. Frankly, I get a little weary of being warned not to "rush ahead of the Lord." I believe that the disciples were in a hurry to get the job done. They were not in a panic, in a frenzy, in a mad rush. But, young people, they were *moving* — the book of Acts is the fastest-moving book in the New Testament. True, they waited on God (and much of their waiting they did at night, while our dear brethren—who like to give this advice today— get their regular eight hours of beauty sleep). But *after* they waited on God they moved out into action for Him. Let us beware of a life which is busy but barren. May we continue to strive for efficiency and speed in accomplishing our routine tasks for Him. Every minute we save in accomplishing these tasks is a minute we can spend in direct evangelism.

And now, we will meet the last pseudo-disciple, **Mr. Status-Seeker.** He is driven by a great desire for position and importance. He wants to be

known as a man of God; he wants to be known as a great preacher, a great Bible teacher, a great organizer. He wants a special title which he can nail on the door of his private office. And it is all a sham to God. Recognition of man . . . what is it? In the sight of God—*nothing!*

America is a nation of status seekers, and status seeking has so infiltrated American Christendom that we hardly know how to accept a person for what he is. And the majority of the world follows close behind in this frantic quest for recognition. The famous book, *The Status Seekers*, by Vance Packard, shows how the people of the world are status seekers. But how deadly it is when this same motivation comes into our Christian service. How often we treat a man kindly because we want something from him or because he has a certain status. How unreal that is — how God must hate it.

Young people, what are the titles given to the Lord Jesus Christ? *Servant, Man of Sorrows, Man acquainted with grief, Foot-washer, Lamb of God.* These are His titles. And His status symbol? Well, he never got a university degree. He didn't have a private office, nor a secretary, nor an expense account. No! His only status symbol was the *Cross.* Do you want more, young person? Do you feel a little out of place because you have no status, no official position? Do you want to stop being a "nobody" and become a "somebody"? Well, then, don't say you want to be a follower of Jesus, because He *was* a Somebody—but He became a Nobody! He, "being in the form of God . . . made Himself of no reputation . . ." (Phil. 2:6,7). Oh, may God deliver us from this curse of our day, this craving for recognition and praise of men. *May our only claim be that we are "accepted in the Beloved"* (Eph. 1:6).

Well, after all this, I can hear you saying to yourself, "That finishes me. I'm going home. I realize I am a phony. Who can live up to that?"

Just a minute, please, and let me say this: Nobody can live up to it! *Nobody!* The only answer then is the *all-sufficiency of Christ.* Admit that you are a sinner. Admit that you are a failure. Come to the Cross of Christ and allow His life to take over in you. After all this you would think we would all be walking on the Calvary Road, wouldn't you? You would think we would be going to our friends, our wives, our husbands, our leaders, in brokenness and repentance. "I lost my patience with you. I'm sorry. Please forgive me. . . . Look, brother, I shouldn't have said that. I've sinned against you."

We are not going to have communion with God if we are always pretending, pretending, pretending. Why are we afraid to come to the light, to the cross, to each other with our wretched sinful lives? It is our only hope! Do you know, after some messages, the ones who come to me in brokenness are the ones who are walking closest to the Cross! Often they are leaders in this work. I know they are living for the Lord. I know they are walking with Him. . . and yet they come in repentance because He has convicted them on some point or other in their lives. After the message on "Hunger for God," I received a letter from one of the leaders who is probably doing more than most . . . and he was absolutely broken to tears and repentance.

Oh, for more like this! Men and women who will not harden their hearts, not even on some minor point, but will bend and break and walk in daily revival. If you have sinned against some brother, or offended him in any way, there is only one course for you and that is to go in humility and say, "Forgive me."

I pray that no one will go on from here without knowing the reality of being broken and cleansed before the Lord. You might be a leader, you might be a pastor. But I tell you, the *only place* of grace and blessing is at the foot of the Cross of Christ. He will cleanse you, and as you go out into this newness of life, whenever the Spirit speaks to you about something, whenever you find any of these twenty-one little men or women moving into your life, immediately you must repent and turn to Christ, and realize that He cleanses from these areas of sin. *But do not hide it! Do not bury it! Do not let your pride keep you from confessing it.* Let us stay at the foot of the Cross where the blood of Christ cleanses from all sin!

THERE'S A PLACE FOR YOU!

For more information concerning short or long term mission projects, or to obtain a catalog of literature currently available please write or call:

LITERATURE

P.O Box 1047
Waynesboro, GA, 30830, USA
ph: (706)554-5827
Fax: (706)554-7444
postmaster@omlit.om.org